Leaves

David Ezra Stein

McGraw Hill Education

mhreadingwonders.com

Copyright ©2007 by David Ezra Stein.
Published by arrangement with G. P. Putnam's Sons,
a division of Penguin Young Readers Group,
a member of Penguin Group (USA) Inc.
All rights reserved.

No part of this publication may be reproduced
or distributed in any form or by an means,
or stored in a database or retrieval system, without the
prior written consent of McGraw-Hill Education,
including, but not limited to, network storage or
transmission, or broadcast for distance learning.

Send all inquiries to:
McGraw-Hill Education
Two Penn Plaza
New York NY 10121

ISBN: 978-0-07-678760-9
MHID: 0-07-678760-5

Printed in China

9 10 11 12 13 DSS 28 27 26 25 24

For my mother,
a bear of great heart
and an exceptional human being.

It was his first year.

Everything

was going well

until the first leaf fell.

"Are you okay?" he wondered.

Then . . . a red one fell,
a yellow one fell,

all over his island, the leaves
were falling.

He tried to catch them
and put them back on . . .

but it was not the same.

He sat beneath a tree
and watched them go, all around.

But he grew sleepy,
and so . . .

he found a hole

and filled it with leaves,

and went to sleep,

just as the wind began to blow.

Winter came.

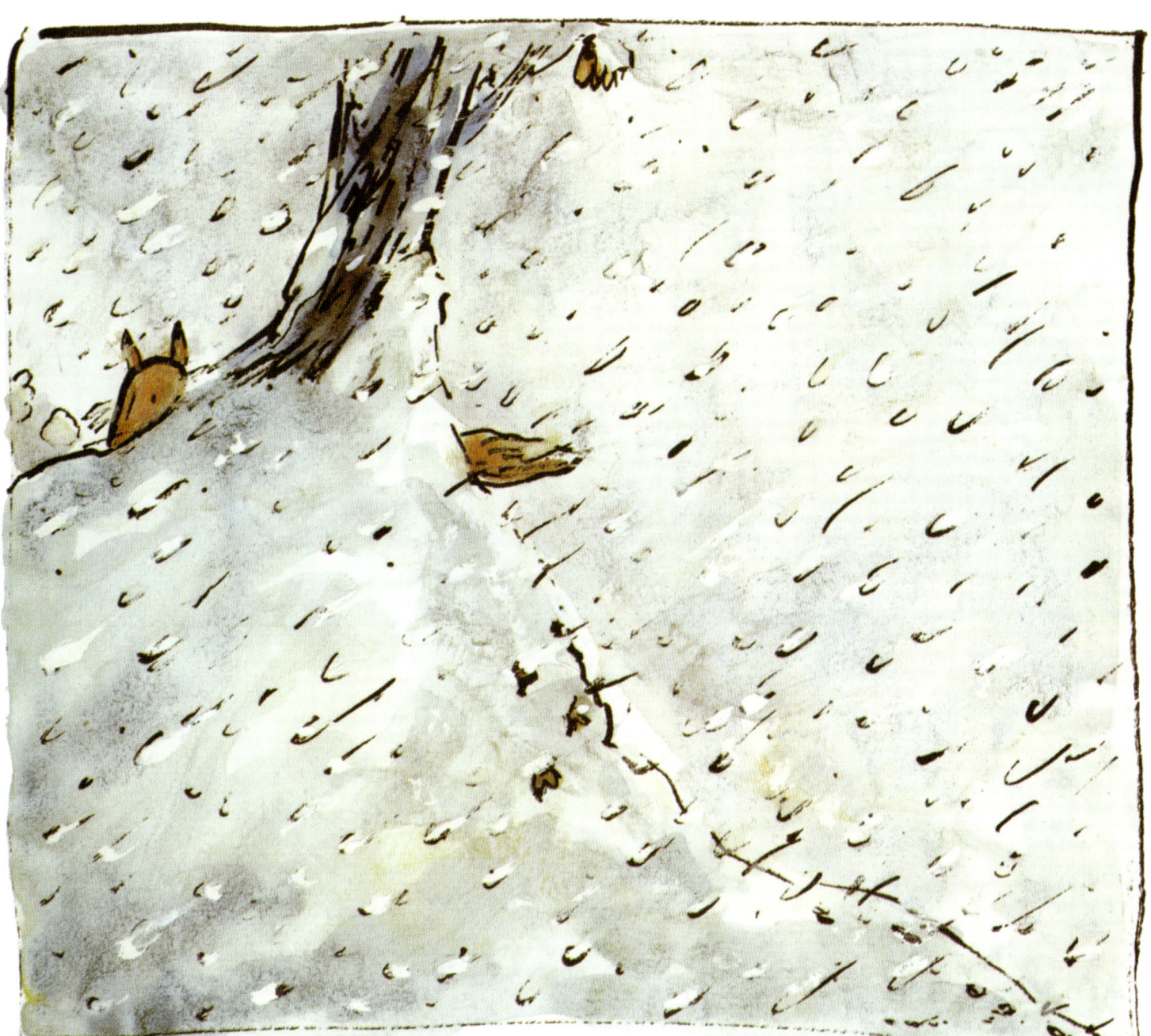

He slept, snug in the ground,

while the snow piled thick.

In the spring,

with wide eyes, he woke.

He felt the sun

and saw the little buds on the bare arms of the trees

and the tiny leaves that had begun to unfold.

"Welcome!" he cried.

And, he thought, the leaves welcomed him.